THE FABULOUS LOST & FOUND

AND THE LITTLE MOUSE WHO SPOKE LATIN

WRITTEN BY MARK PALLIS
ILLUSTRATED BY PETER BAYNTON

NEU WESTEND
— PRESS —

For Emily and Lucy. Legends! - MP

For Hannah and Skye - PB

THE FABULOUS LOST & FOUND AND THE LITTLE MOUSE WHO SPOKE LATIN

First Printing, 2020
ISBN 978-1-913595-01-2
NeuWestendPress.com

THE FABULOUS LOST & FOUND

AND THE LITTLE MOUSE WHO SPOKE LATIN

WRITTEN BY MARK PALLIS
ILLUSTRATED BY PETER BAYNTON

NEU WESTEND
— PRESS —

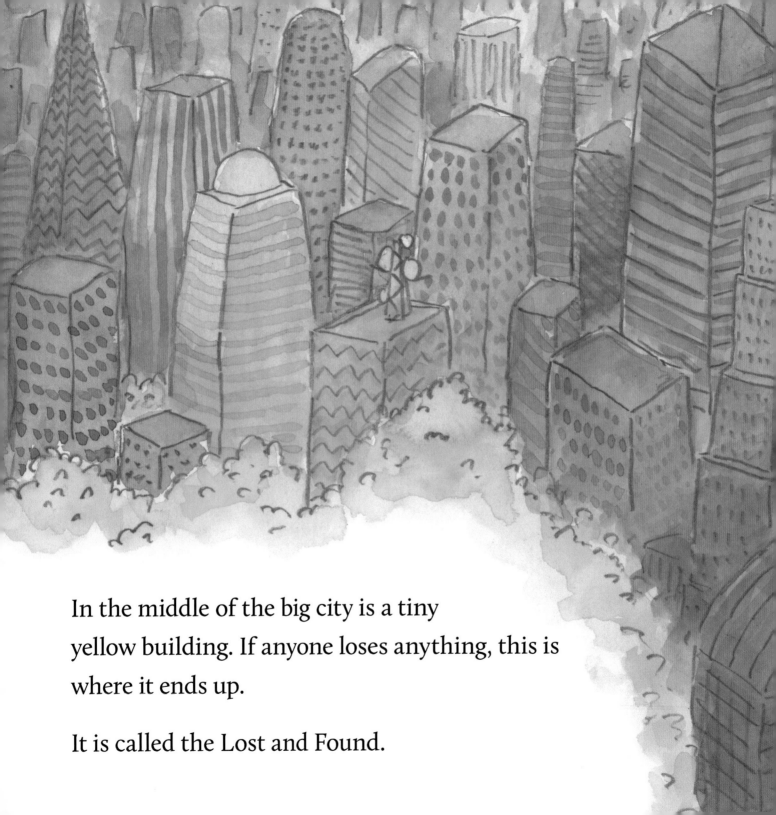

In the middle of the big city is a tiny
yellow building. If anyone loses anything, this is
where it ends up.

It is called the Lost and Found.

Mr and Mrs Frog keep everything safe, hoping that someday every lost watch and bag and phone and toy and shoe and cheesegrater will find its owner again.

But the shop is very small. And there are so many lost things. It is all quite a squeeze, but still, it's fabulous.

One sunny day, a little mouse walked in.

"Welcome," said Mrs Frog. "What have you lost?"

"Amisi meum galerum," said the mouse.

Mr and Mrs Frog could not speak Latin. They had no idea what the little mouse was saying.

What shall we do? they wondered.

Maybe she's lost an umbrella. Everyone loses an umbrella at least twice, thought Mr Frog.

"Have you lost this?" asked Mr Frog.

"Non umbraculum," replied the mouse.

Then Mrs Frog remembered something
that had been handed in a few months ago...

"Is this yours?" Mrs Frog asked, holding up a chunk of cheese.

"Non caseus. Putet!" said the mouse.

"Time to put that cheese in the bin dear," said Mr Frog.

"Maybe the word 'galerum' means coat," said Mr Frog.

"Now where did I put that nice yellow one?"

"Got it!" said Mr Frog.

Non vitra ocularia.

Non calcei.

"Amisi meum galerum," said
the mouse.

Non duae birotae.

Non abacus.

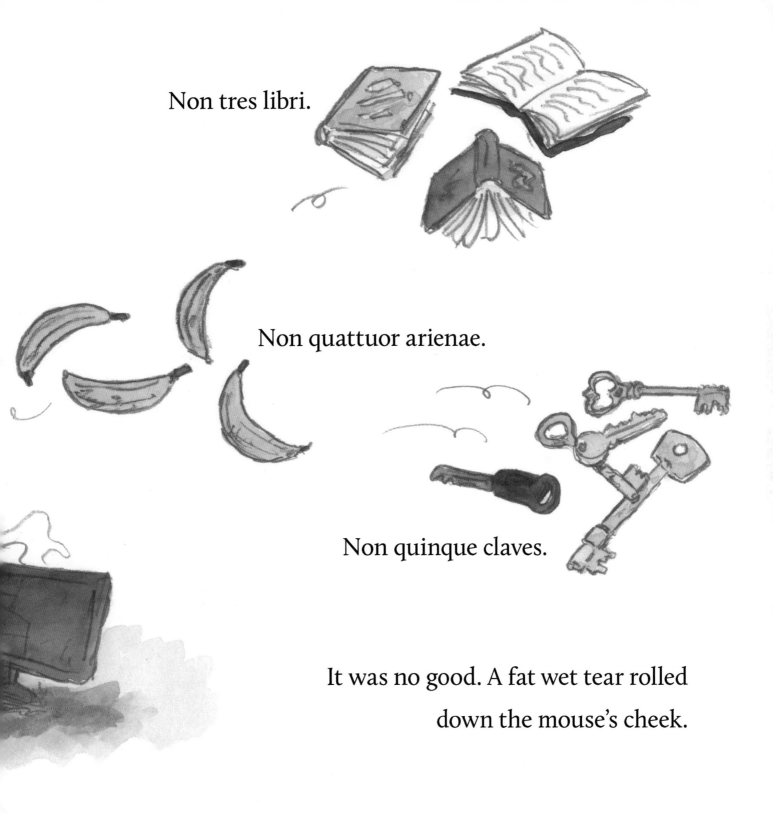

Non tres libri.

Non quattuor arienae.

Non quinque claves.

It was no good. A fat wet tear rolled
down the mouse's cheek.

"How about a nice cup of tea?" asked Mrs Frog kindly.

"Herbiferum potum amo. Gratias ago," replied the mouse.
They sat together, sipping their tea and all feeling a bit sad.

Non rubrum.

Non flavum.

Non badium.

Non viride.

Non varium.

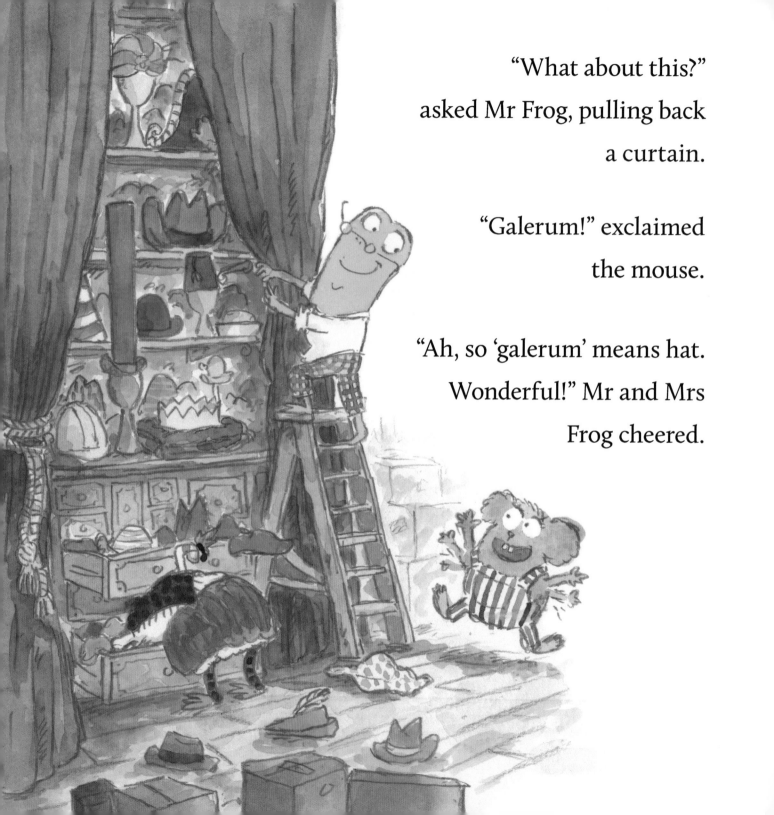

"What about this?"
asked Mr Frog, pulling back
a curtain.

"Galerum!" exclaimed
the mouse.

"Ah, so 'galerum' means hat.
Wonderful!" Mr and Mrs
Frog cheered.

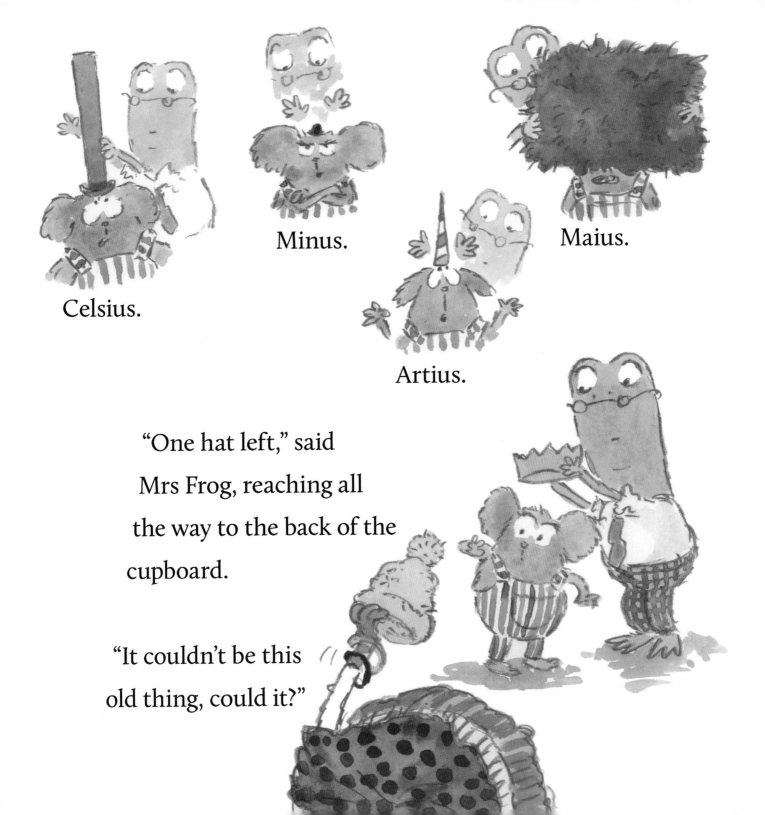

Celsius.

Minus.

Artius.

Maius.

"One hat left," said Mrs Frog, reaching all the way to the back of the cupboard.

"It couldn't be this old thing, could it?"

"Meum galerum.

Meum galerum inveni!

Multas gratias tibi ago," said the mouse.

And just like that, the mouse found her hat.

"Vale," she said, as she skipped away.
"Vale," replied Mr and Mrs Frog.

"I wonder who will come tomorrow?" said Mr Frog.
Mrs Frog put her arm around him.

"I don't know," she replied, giving him a squeeze,
"but whoever it is, we'll do our best to help."

LEARNING TO LOVE LANGUAGES

An additional language opens a child's mind, broadens their horizons and enriches their emotional life. Research has shown that the time between a child's birth and their sixth or seventh birthday is a "golden period" when they are most receptive to new languages. This is because they have an in-built ability to distinguish the sounds they hear and make sense of them. The Story-powered Language Learning Method taps into these natural abilities.

HOW THE STORY-POWERED LANGUAGE LEARNING METHOD WORKS

We create an emotionally engaging and funny story for children and adults to enjoy together, just like any other picture book. Studies show that social interaction, like enjoying a book together, is critical in language learning.

Through the story, we introduce a relatable character who speaks only in the new language. This helps build empathy and a positive attitude towards people who speak different languages. These are both important aspects in laying the foundations for lasting language acquisition in a child's life.

As the story progresses, the child naturally works with the characters to discover the meanings of a wide range of fun new words. Strategic use of humour ensures that this subconscious learning is rewarded with laughter; the child feels good and the first seeds of a lifelong love of languages are sown.

For more information and free downloads visit www.neuwestendpress.com

ALL THE BEAUTIFUL LATIN WORDS AND PHRASES FROM OUR STORY

amisi meum galerum	I've lost my hat
umbraculum	an umbrella
caseus	cheese
putet	it stinks
amiculum	coat
amictorium	scarf
bracae	trousers
vitra ocularia	sunglasses
diplois (greek)	cloak (jumper)
calcei	shoes
unus	one
duo (duae)	two
tres	three
quattuor	four
quinque	five
abacus	counting device (computer!)
libri	books
claves	keys
arienae	bananas
birotae	two wheeled chariots (bicycles!)
herbiferum potum amo	I love herbal drink (tea)
gratias ago	thank you
non	no

multas gratias tibi ago	thank you very much
capillamentum	wig
rubrum	red
flavum	blond
badium	brown
viride	green
varium	multicoloured
celsius	too tall
maius	too big
minus	too small
artius	too tight
meum galerum inveni	I've found my hat
vale	goodbye

THE WORLD OF
THE FABULOUS LOST & FOUND

THIS STORY IS ALSO AVAILABLE IN...

FRENCH

SPANISH

ITALIAN

CZECH

KOREAN

WELSH

GERMAN

HEBREW

SWEDISH

POLISH

SLOVAKIAN

VIETNAMESE

TAGALOG

PORTUGUESE

...AND MANY MORE LANGUAGES!

ENJOYED IT?
WRITE A REVIEW AND
LET US KNOW!

@MARK_PALLIS ON TWITTER
WWW.MARKPALLIS.COM

@PETERBAYNTON ON INSTAGRAM
WWW.PETERBAYNTON.COM

Printed in Great Britain
by Amazon